Bergen's Best Bridge Quizzes

Volume 1

By Marty Bergen

Bergen Books

Thanks To:

Layout, cover design, and editing by
Hammond Graphics.

My very special thanks to: Cheryl Angel, Cheryl Bergen,
Gary Blaiss, Trish and John L. Block, Ollie Burno,
Pete Filandro, Jim Garnher, Terry Gerber,
Lynn and Steve Gerhard, Steve Jones, Doris Katz,
Danny Kleinman, Harriet and David Morris,
Phyllis Nicholson, Mary and Richard Oshlag,
Helene Pittler, Sally and Dave Porter, David Pollard,
Mark Raphaelson, Jesse Reisman, Carl Ritner, John Rudy,
Eric Sandberg, Maggie Sparrow, Merle Stetser,
and Bobby Stinebaugh.

Bergen Books
9 River Chase Terrace
Palm Beach Gardens, FL 33418-6817

First Edition published 2003.
Printed in the United States of America.
10 9 8 7 6 5 4 3 2 1

First Printing: October, 2003

Library of Congress Control Number: 2003097068

ISBN: 0-9744714-0-2

Bridge Books by Marty Bergen

To Open, or Not to Open

Better Rebidding with Bergen

Hand Evaluation: Points, Schmoints!

Understanding 1NT Forcing

Marty Sez

Marty Sez...Volume 2

Marty Sez...Volume 3

POINTS SCHMOINTS!

More POINTS SCHMOINTS!

Introduction to Negative Doubles

Negative Doubles

Better Bidding with Bergen, Volume I

Better Bidding with Bergen, Volume II

Everyone's Guide to the New Convention Card

FYI

The player with the bidding decision to make is indicated by three question marks: ???

For consistency, South is always that player, and his hand is the one displayed.

Every bidding diagram begins with West.

West	North	East	South
—	—	—	2♡
All Pass			

The dashes are place holders, and in the example above, show that the auction did not begin with West, North, or East. The dealer was South.

The "—" does not indicate a "Pass."

CONTENTS

Stop – Read This

Welcome to my new series, *Bergen's Best Bridge Quizzes (BBBQ)*. I hope you are as excited about it as I am. Inspired by many requests, this will be the first of many such "test your skills" books. All of these will feature quizzes based on an assortment of practical topics.

Each chapter will deal with a specific auction and provide 10 hands for you to decide what to bid. I urge you to think about each hand as if you were actually "at the table," and to write down your action before reading on.

In addition to the bidding quizzes, each chapter contains a separate quiz on card-play. Some of these non-bidding quizzes deal with declarer play, others focus on defense, and one quiz gives you the opportunity to make the killing opening lead. Each of these card-play quizzes consists of several questions, which are then answered in detail.

When you arrive at chapter 7, don't be thrown by the title, "OBAR-BIDS." This is merely another name for "pre-balancing" and is very carefully explained.

Stop – Read This

I've tried to explain my answers as thoroughly and helpfully as possible. If you like, you can grade yourself by awarding 10 points for each correct answer. Of course, you may decide that you are right and I am wrong, and that you scored 100 while I only scored 70. Fair enough!

Although everyone loves to get good grades, how you scored is not the key. All that matters is what you know *afterwards,* and how you apply what you've learned when you play bridge.

Does it matter if you're playing matchpoint duplicate, team of four, or rubber bridge? Not at all. I recommend every bid, play, and lead described in this book regardless of the form of scoring.

I wanted this book to test your judgment, rather than your knowledge of conventions. The agreements in BBBQ1 are as follows: 1NT = 15-17 HCP, Jacoby Transfers, Negative Doubles, and Standard leads and signals.

For your convenience, a complete listing and description of all conventions that appear in the chapters can be found in the Glossary Plus.

Stop – Read This

Do not overlook the back of the book. These four segments *do* provide valuable information. Segments I-III also include page numbers to allow you to find where they originally appeared. They are:

I. Bergenisms
These concise, carefully-worded statements can be an invaluable aid to the reader in countless situations.

II. Glossary Plus
A very thorough explanation of conventions and terms used in BBBQ1 that may not be familiar to all players.

III. Calling All Cue-Bids
A complete listing and explanation of all the cue-bids found in this book.

IIII. To Alert or Not to Alert
A must-read for everyone who plays duplicate. This page will clarify which bids and doubles presented in BBBQ1 need to be alerted. Every bid or double that *might* be alertable is listed.

Rebidding After a Transfer

For each of the hands below, the auction has begun:

West	North	East	South
—	1NT	Pass	2♡*
Pass	2♠	Pass	???
	*Jacoby Transfer		

On this auction, if you bid a new suit, it's game-forcing.

As South, evaluate each hand and decide what to do. Both sides are vulnerable.

1.   ♠ J 7 5 4 2   ♡ J 6 4   ◇ K J 10 9 5   ♣ —

2.   ♠ A 9 7 5 4   ♡ A 5 4   ◇ 10 7 4 2   ♣ 5

3.   ♠ A K 10 7 3   ♡ 8 4   ◇ K Q 9 8   ♣ 8 5

4.   ♠ Q 8 6 4 2   ♡ K 4   ◇ K Q 9 8   ♣ Q J

5.   ♠ K J 10 8 4   ♡ 6 4   ◇ A K 5   ♣ A 10 8

6.   ♠ K 7 6 4 2   ♡ K Q   ◇ K J 2   ♣ Q J 6

7.   ♠ A Q 9 6 3 2   ♡ J 9 5   ◇ 8 5 2   ♣ 3

8.   ♠ A 8 7 5 4 3   ♡ 8 5   ◇ 2   ♣ A K 10 8

9.   ♠ K Q 9 7 6 5   ♡ A 6 5   ◇ 8   ♣ K 10 2

10.   ♠ A J 9 8 5   ♡ A J   ◇ 10 6 5 2   ♣ A K

Rebidding After a Transfer

West	North	East	South
—	1NT	Pass	2♡*
Pass	2♠	Pass	???

*Jacoby Transfer

1.   ♠ J 7 5 4 2 ♡ J 6 4 ◇ K J 10 9 5 ♣ —
Pass. With no assurance of a spade fit, you'd better stay low. If opener had four spades and a nice hand, he would have "super-accepted" by jumping to 3♠ and you would have been delighted to bid game.

2.   ♠ A 9 7 5 4 ♡ A 5 4 ◇ 10 7 4 2 ♣ 5
Bid 2NT. You don't like bidding notrump with a singleton, but no other bid shows an invitational hand and a 5-card spade suit.

3.   ♠ A K 10 7 3 ♡ 8 4 ◇ K Q 9 8 ♣ 8 5
Bid 3◇. You're not eager to play in 5◇, but there's no reason to suppress your second suit. This bid gives partner valuable information about your distribution and where your strength is located. If opener has fewer than three spades, but is weak in hearts or clubs, your 3◇ bid will be helpful in selecting the best contract.

4.   ♠ Q 8 6 4 2 ♡ K 4 ◇ K Q 9 8 ♣ Q J
Bid 3NT. Same distribution as the previous hand; but with your scattered strength, you're content to give opener a choice between 3NT and 4♠.

5.　　♠ K J 10 8 4　♡ 6 4　◇ A K 5　♣ A 10 8
Bid 4NT. With strong spades and nice outside honors,
this is an upgradable hand. Slam is quite possible.
The 4NT bid is *not* Blackwood. It is "quantitative,"
and means that you are inviting partner to go to slam
if he has a maximum for his 1NT bid. He will usually
choose either pass, 6♠, or 6NT; but he can also
introduce a worthwhile suit of his own.

6.　　♠ K 7 6 4 2　♡ K Q　◇ K J 2　♣ Q J 6
Bid 3NT. With weak spades and not-so-nice outside
honors, downgrade this hand and forget about slam.

7.　　♠ A Q 9 6 3 2　♡ J 9 5　◇ 8 5 2　♣ 3
Bid 3♠, which shows an invitational hand with a
6-card suit and leaves the final decision to partner.

8.　　♠ A 8 7 5 4 3　♡ 8 5　◇ 2　♣ A K 10 8
Bid 3♣, not 4♠. This promising hand has real slam
potential. 6♣ could easily be ice-cold.

9.　　♠ K Q 9 7 6 5　♡ A 6 5　◇ 8　♣ K 10 2
Bid 4◇, assuming that you are playing splinter bids.
Keep in mind: **Not all splinter bids are double jumps.**
This "self-splinter" promises 0-1 diamond and a 6-card
major, and invites 6♠. If opener has a healthy 1NT
with values outside of diamonds, he'll move towards
slam. If you're not playing splinter bids, you would be
forced to choose from some very imperfect options.

West	North	East	South
—	1NT	Pass	2♡*
Pass	2♠	Pass	???

*Jacoby Transfer

10. ♠ A J 9 8 5 ♡ A J ◇ 10 6 5 2 ♣ A K

I could almost write an entire chapter about this hand.

Question: Are you ready to insist on slam?

Answer: Yes. You'd prefer nicer diamonds, but with three aces and a promising 5-card suit, this hand is worth 18 points.

Question: Should you mention diamonds?

Answer: No. Although it is *possible* that 6◇ is your best contract, introducing *this* suit is going too far.

Question: Should you be interested in a grand slam?

Answer: No. Partner may have the perfect hand for seven, but be realistic; just get to the best small slam.

Question: What should you bid?

Answer: 5NT, asking opener to choose a small slam. I recommend "5NT, pick a slam" to every player.

Question: What should opener bid after your 5NT?

Answer: If he has 2 spades, he will bid 6NT. With 3 or 4 spades, he should bid 6♠.

North

Contract: 4♠
Lead: ♥Q

♠ 10 9 6 5 4 3
♥ K 7 4
◇ 8
♣ J 6 4

South
♠ K Q J 2
♥ A 9 6
◇ J 10 5 2
♣ A Q

West	North	East	South
—	—	—	1NT
Pass	2♥*	Pass	3♠
Pass	4♠	All Pass	

*Jacoby Transfer

North had not planned to bid again, but took a second look at his 6-card suit and singleton after South jumped.

Question 1: How many losers do you have?

Question 2: Can you still make the hand if West has the ♣K?

Question 3: In which hand will you win the opening heart lead?

Question 4: What do you lead at trick 2?

Question 1: How many losers do you have?

Answer: You have 4 possible losers – one in each suit.

Question 2: Can you still make the hand if West has the ♣K?

Answer: Absolutely. You don't need to rely on the club finesse. Instead. you should set up dummy's ♣J. Once you do, you can use it to discard your heart loser.

Question 3: In which hand will you win the opening heart lead?

Answer: In your hand. You *must* save dummy's ♡K so that you will have an immediate entry to the board to cash the ♣J once it is good. **When declarer has a choice of where to win a trick, think carefully about where you'll need to be *later on*.**

Question 4: What do you lead at trick 2?

Answer: Lead the ♣A to unblock. Now, continue by sacrificing the ♣Q. West can win his king, but dummy is looking good. You will get to the board with the ♡K and discard your last heart on the established ♣J.

Rebidding After a Transfer

Here is the entire deal:

North

Contract: 4♠
Lead: ♡Q

♠ 10 9 6 5 4 3
♡ K 7 4
◇ 8
♣ J 6 4

West

♠ 8 7
♡ Q J 10 2
◇ A Q 9 3
♣ K 9 7

East

♠ A
♡ 8 5 3
◇ K 7 6 4
♣ 10 8 5 3 2

South

♠ K Q J 2
♡ A 9 6
◇ J 10 5 2
♣ A Q

West	North	East	South
—	—	—	1NT
Pass	2♡*	Pass	3♠
Pass	4♠	All Pass	

*Jacoby Transfer

West	North	East	South
Pass	1♢	Pass	1♡
Pass	1♠	Pass	???

What do you know about North's hand? He would have opened 1♢ on a 3-card suit *only* if he had precisely 4 spades, 4 hearts and 2 clubs. When North didn't raise hearts, he couldn't have four of them. Therefore, on this auction, he must have 4+ diamonds.

North's 1♠ bid is not forcing; but because he needs 19 HCP to jump-shift, he could have as many as 18.

As South, evaluate each hand and decide what to do. Neither side is vulnerable.

1. ♠ 7 5 3 ♡ K 8 7 5 4 ♢ A Q 5 ♣ 4 2
2. ♠ 5 4 3 2 ♡ Q J 9 7 ♢ 9 8 ♣ K J 3
3. ♠ Q J 9 7 ♡ 9 8 3 2 ♢ K J 3 ♣ 3 2
4. ♠ K Q 9 ♡ A 8 6 4 2 ♢ 6 ♣ 6 4 3 2
5. ♠ Q 5 ♡ 9 7 6 3 2 ♢ A Q ♣ 6 4 3 2
6. ♠ K 7 5 ♡ A Q 7 5 3 ♢ K Q ♣ 7 6 2
7. ♠ 6 3 2 ♡ K Q 5 4 ♢ 9 6 4 ♣ A Q 9
8. ♠ 9 8 6 5 ♡ K Q J 10 9 7 ♢ 7 ♣ 8 3
9. ♠ J 7 4 3 ♡ Q J 6 5 2 ♢ A 2 ♣ K 3
10. ♠ A 10 9 3 ♡ A K 5 4 2 ♢ 9 5 ♣ 6 4

We Bid Three Suits

West	North	East	South
Pass	1◇	Pass	1♡
Pass	1♠	Pass	???

1. ♠ 7 5 3 ♡ K 8 7 5 4 ◇ A Q 5 ♣ 4 2

Bid 2◇. If North has a maximum for his auction, 3NT is still quite possible. If he has three hearts, you'd love to end up in that suit, possibly in game. If he has neither, a 2◇ contract will still be okay, even if it is only a 4-3 fit.

2. ♠ 5 4 3 2 ♡ Q J 9 7 ◇ 9 8 ♣ K J 3

Pass, despite finding a spade fit. Before the auction began, you had a lousy hand. When partner showed diamonds and spades, the value of your four honors in clubs and hearts decreased significantly. In a spade contract, you will contribute *no* high cards in either of partner's suits. I've also seen better trump support.

3. ♠ Q J 9 7 ♡ 9 8 3 2 ◇ K J 3 ♣ 3 2

Bid 2♠. Location, location, location. All four of your honor cards are located in partner's suits, where they are certain to be useful (proven values). *This* hand is worth a lot more than 7 HCP (and a doubleton).

4. ♠ K Q 9 ♡ A 8 6 4 2 ◇ 6 ♣ 6 4 3 2

Bid 2♠. Raising partner's 4-card spade suit with only
3 trumps is far from ideal, but with no club stopper and
a singleton, neither is 1NT. Rebidding 2♡ with *this* suit
has no appeal. Your hand is too promising to give up on
game, so pass is out. In a spade contract, your singleton
diamond, two spade honors and ♡A are all assets that
should compensate for the missing trump.

5. ♠ Q 5 ♡ 9 7 6 3 2 ◇ A Q ♣ 6 4 3 2

Bid 1NT. A very imperfect hand, but you don't have a
reasonable alternative. When your partnership has bid
three suits, you shouldn't bid notrump without a stopper
in the fourth suit. The *only* exception is: at responder's
second turn, if stuck for a bid, he can make a 1NT fib.

6. ♠ K 7 5 ♡ A Q 7 5 3 ◇ K Q ♣ 7 6 2

Bid 2♣. Fortunately, responder *does* have alternatives
with a strong hand. **The use of the fourth suit as an
artificial, forcing bid should be an important part of
every responder's repertoire.** It gives opener the
chance to describe his hand further. His first priority is
to show 3-card support for your major, but he will also
be eager to bid notrump with a stopper in the fourth
suit. Is responder's bid of the 4th suit game-forcing?
I firmly answer "yes," while others believe, equally
firmly, that it is not. Every partnership must resolve
this one way or the other.

West	North	East	South
Pass	1♦	Pass	1♡
Pass	1♠	Pass	???

7.　♠ 6 3 2　♡ K Q 5 4　♦ 9 6 4　♣ A Q 9

Bid 2NT to invite game. **If your partnership treats all jumps as forcing, you have no way to invite.** With invitational hands, responder should jump, but with game-forcing hands, he should bid the fourth suit (or jump to game when he is sure of the best contract).

8.　♠ 9 8 6 5　♡ K Q J 10 9 7　♦ 7　♣ 8 3

Bid 2♡, despite your 4-card spade support. If hearts are trump, this heart suit will produce five sure tricks. If spades are trump, the value of your heart suit is very much in doubt because of your lack of entries. **With an independent major suit, don't even consider other contracts.**

9.　♠ J 7 4 3　♡ Q J 6 5 2　♦ A 2　♣ K 3

Bid 3♠. Your honors in clubs and hearts are not well-located, and your spades are weak. **When you have weak trumps and only an 8-card fit, you should be cautious.** If partner declines your invitation, you'll have no regrets.

10.　♠ A 10 9 3　♡ A K 5 4 2　♦ 9 5　♣ 6 4

Bid 4♠. The same distribution and 11 HCP as the previous hand, but with 3 quick tricks and strong trumps, you are ready to insist on game.

West (You)	*North*	*East*	*South*
Pass	1◇	Pass	1♡
Pass	1♠	Pass	2◇
Pass	3♡	Pass	4♡
All Pass			

As West, you hold:

♠ A 10 8 3   ♡ A 3   ◇ 8 7 3 2   ♣ J 10 8

After an interesting N–S auction, you find yourself on lead against 4♡.

Question 1: What do you know about North's shape?

Question 2: Based on the N-S bidding, what do you know about your partner's distribution?

Question 3: Do you see prospects for four tricks?

S, H, D, C

Question 4: What card would you lead?

By the way: When you are playing "real bridge," do you ask yourself questions 1-3 (above) before making an opening lead? I hope so.

Question 1: What do you know about North's shape?

Answer: 1♠ showed four spades – that's easy.
His jump to 3♡ had to be based on three hearts and
a very strong distributional hand, so North must be short
in clubs. Because he has 0-1 club, he must have at least
five diamonds.

Question 2: Based on the N-S bidding, what do you
know about your partner's distribution?

Answer: The opponent's bidding indicates at least 8
diamonds, so with your 4 cards, **partner must have a
singleton or void.** As for hearts, South would not have
bid 2♢ if he had a 6-card heart suit, so East has 3.

Question 3: Do you see prospects for four tricks?

Answer: Definitely. Just lead diamonds at every
opportunity. With two fast entries (♡A and ♠A),
you will get in twice and can give partner two ruffs.
In fact, it would not have been crazy to double 4♡.

Question 4: What card would you lead?

Answer: The ♢8. This is a suit-preference situation,
so lead your highest diamond to tell partner that your
entry is in spades, the higher-ranking side suit.

We Bid Three Suits

Here is the entire deal:

Contract: 4♡
Lead: ◇8

North
♠ K 5 4 2
♡ K Q 9
◇ A J 10 5 4
♣ A

West (You)
♠ A 10 8 3
♡ A 3
◇ 8 7 3 2
♣ J 10 8

East
♠ Q J 9 6
♡ 6 4 2
◇ 6
♣ Q 9 7 6 3

South
♠ 7
♡ J 10 8 7 5
◇ K Q 9
♣ K 5 4 2

West (You)	North	East	South
Pass	1◇	Pass	1♡
Pass	1♠	Pass	2◇
Pass	3♡	Pass	4♡
All Pass			

AFTER OPENER RAISES YOUR MAJOR

For each of the hands below, the auction has begun:

West	North	East	South
—	1♦	Pass	1♠
Pass	2♠	Pass	???

Keep in mind that North might have only 3 spades. On some hands, he should be delighted to raise with 3-card support. On others, he will raise because there are no alternatives. Here are examples of both:

♠ A K Q   ♡ x x   ◇ A x x x x   ♣ x x x

♠ J x x   ♡ A K x x   ◇ A x x x x   ♣ x

As South, evaluate each hand and decide what to do. Only your side is vulnerable.

1.   ♠ 9 5 3 2   ♡ K Q J   ◇ A   ♣ J 8 7 4 2

2.   ♠ Q 8 5 2   ♡ K Q 9   ◇ J 8 5   ♣ A K J

3.   ♠ K 9 5 3   ♡ 5 3   ◇ A K J   ♣ Q J 10 8

4.   ♠ A K J 10   ♡ A 6 5   ◇ J 9 7 6   ♣ 3 2

5.   ♠ A 10 7 6 4 2   ♡ 8 3   ◇ K Q   ♣ A 10 3

6.   ♠ K 8 7 6 5 3   ♡ A 7 5 3   ◇ 8 2   ♣ 5

7.   ♠ K 9 4 3   ♡ A Q 6   ◇ 10 7   ♣ Q 9 5 3

8.   ♠ A Q J 6 4   ♡ K 10   ◇ J 5 4   ♣ 6 4 3

9.   ♠ 7 6 4 3 2   ♡ A K 10   ◇ 10 5   ♣ A Q J

10.   ♠ A J 9 7 5 3   ♡ 9   ◇ K 9 4   ♣ A 7 3

After Opener Raises Your Major

West	North	East	South
—	1♦	Pass	1♠
Pass	2♠	Pass	???

1.   ♠ 9 5 3 2   ♡ K Q J   ♦ A   ♣ J 8 7 4 2
Pass. I *hate* this hand. Why?

- First and foremost, the anemic trumps.
  Marty Sez: With bad trumps, tread lightly.

- Your 5-card suit is very weak.

- The singleton in partner's suit is a liability when
  your side declares.

- Almost all of your strength is concentrated in
  your two shorter suits.

2.   ♠ Q 8 5 2   ♡ K Q 9   ♦ J 8 5   ♣ A K J
Bid 3NT. If partner has four spades, he'll bid 4♠.
If he has only three, he will pass. Voilà.

3.   ♠ K 9 5 3   ♡ 5 3   ♦ A K J   ♣ Q J 10 8
Bid 3♣. You're strong enough to insist on game, but
with only a fair 4-card suit, jumping to 4♠ would be
premature. This flexible bid is forcing for one round,
and preserves all options. Depending on partner's
hand, your possible game contracts include spades,
notrump, diamonds, and even clubs.

4.　　♠ A K J 10　♡ A 6 5　◇ J 9 7 6　♣ 3 2
Bid 4♠. With *these* spades, you're ready, willing, and able to declare 4♠ even if opener has only three.

5.　　♠ A 10 7 6 4 2　♡ 8 3　◇ K Q　♣ A 10 3
Bid 3♣ for now. *Do not* make the lazy bid of 4♠. Your diamond honors, two aces, and 6-card suit combine to give you definite slam potential.

6.　　♠ K 8 7 6 5 3　♡ A 7 5 3　◇ 8 2　♣ 5
Bid 4♠. After partner raises, I absolutely, positively love this modest hand. Why?

- Once partner promises spade support, your indifferent 6-card suit is looking a lot better.

- Hands with 6-4 distribution are especially powerful when the partnership has a fit. Your ♡3 is worth *a lot more* than if it was the ◇3 or the ♣3.

- Your singleton is *not* in partner's suit.

- Both honor cards are *proven* values. Honors in the trump suit are virtually guaranteed to be worthwhile, and aces are....ACES. If the hand contained the ♠A and ♡K instead of the actual ♠K and ♡A, the hand would not be as good, because the ♡K is not proven.

West	North	East	South
—	1♢	Pass	1♠
Pass	2♠	Pass	???

7.   ♠ K 9 4 3   ♡ A Q 6   ♢ 10 7   ♣ Q 9 5 3

Bid 2NT, natural and invitational. If opener has four spades, he'll bid 3♠ with a minimum hand, or 4♠ with a bit more. If he has three spades, he can pass, raise to 3NT, or even bid a suit with a very shapely hand.

8.   ♠ A Q J 6 4   ♡ K 10   ♢ J 5 4   ♣ 6 4 3

Bid 3♠, which invites game and should promise a 5-card suit. If opener has three spades, this agreement will reassure him that you *do* have an 8-card fit. With a nice hand, partner can go on to 4♠ without worrying about supporting you with only three spades.

9.   ♠ 7 6 4 3 2   ♡ A K 10   ♢ 10 5   ♣ A Q J

Bid 3NT, treating the spades like a 4-card suit. With your very weak spade suit and great strength in hearts and clubs, you don't need to end up in 4♠ if partner has only three of them.

10.   ♠ A J 9 7 5 3   ♡ 9   ♢ K 9 4   ♣ A 7 3

Bid 4♡. The splinter bid shows 0-1 heart and suggests slam. If opener has most of his values outside of hearts, 6♠ is a definite possibility. If you're not playing splinter bids, you'd bid 3♣ and hope for the best.

Contract: 4♠
Lead: ♣J

North
♠ K Q 10
♡ J 5
♢ K 10 9 7 2
♣ K 7 2

South
♠ J 9 8 5 4
♡ K Q 6
♢ Q J
♣ A 6 4

West	North	East	South
Pass	1♢	Pass	1♠
Pass	2♠	Pass	4♠
All Pass			

Question 1: How many losers do you have?

Question 2: How can you get rid of one of your losers?

Question 3: Should you win the opening club lead in your hand or in the dummy?

Question 4: What would you lead at trick 2?

Question 1: How many losers do you have?

Answer: Four. In addition to the obvious three aces, you're looking at a third-round club loser.

Question 2: How can you get rid of one of your losers?

Answer: After West's club lead, you'll be left with only one club stopper. You *must discard* a club on one of your red-suit winners; therefore, you can't afford to lead trumps first. Both diamonds and hearts have enough honors to get the job done – so how do you choose between them?

Because you don't have the time to draw trumps *first*, you have too many diamonds for your own good! If you work on diamonds, you would need to discard your club loser without getting trumped. However, this will happen *only* if the 6 missing clubs divide 3-3. Don't count on it. But, if you play hearts first, you just need the 8 missing hearts to divide *either* 5-3 or 4-4. Ah – that's much better. Hearts it is. longer shorter suit

Question 3: Should you win the opening club lead in your hand or in the dummy?

Answer: Once you've decided to play hearts, you need to *save* the club entry in the hand which has more hearts (South). Accordingly, win the opening lead with dummy's ♣K.

Question 4: What would you lead at trick 2?

Answer: The ♡J. West can take his ♡A whenever he wants to. You still have the ♣A entry to get to your hand and discard dummy's last club on the third round of hearts. It's now easy to ruff your last club and lead trumps. Your only losers are the three aces.

Here is the entire deal:

North

Contract: 4♠ ♠ K Q 10
Lead: ♣J ♡ J 5
 ◇ K 10 9 7 2
 ♣ K 7 2

West *East*
♠ A 2 ♠ 7 6 3
♡ A 8 7 ♡ 10 9 4 3 2
◇ 8 5 4 3 ◇ A 6
♣ J 10 8 5 ♣ Q 9 3

South
♠ J 9 8 5 4
♡ K Q 6
◇ Q J
♣ A 6 4

West	North	East	South
Pass	1◇	Pass	1♠
Pass	2♠	Pass	4♠
All Pass			

31

OPENER HAS JUMP-SHIFTED

For each of the hands below, the auction has begun:

West	North	East	South
—	1♡	Pass	1♠
Pass	3♣	Pass	???

Opener's *game-forcing* jump-shift shows a very strong unbalanced hand. Many distributions are possible. Opener might have:

> A 2-suiter in hearts and clubs; OR
> 6 or even 7 hearts, possibly with only 3 clubs.

Keep in mind: Regardless of his length in hearts and clubs, opener may have as many as three spades.

As South, evaluate each hand and decide what to do. Both sides are vulnerable.

1.　♠ K J 9 7 5　♡ K　◇ 10 9 5　♣ 7 6 5 3
2.　♠ Q 10 8 7　♡ 7　◇ K J 9 8 6 3　♣ J 4
3.　♠ 9 8 6 4　♡ Q 7　◇ A 6 5 2　♣ Q 6 5
4.　♠ K J 9 5 4　♡ Q 10　◇ 7　♣ 9 8 7 4 3
5.　♠ K Q 9 7 5　♡ A J 6　◇ 8 6　♣ 9 7 4
6.　♠ A 7 5 3　♡ 7　◇ 6 5 2　♣ A J 10 9 7
7.　♠ 9 7 6 4　♡ —　◇ 8 5 3 2　♣ K Q J 7 5
8.　♠ K Q J 10 9 4　♡ K　◇ 8 6 4 3　♣ 7 4
9.　♠ Q 7 6 4 3 2　♡ A Q　◇ 8 5　♣ A Q 9
10.　♠ A Q 7 6 5 3　♡ J　◇ 8 7 5 4　♣ 7 6

West	North	East	South
—	1♡	Pass	1♠
Pass	3♣	Pass	???

1.   ♠ K J 9 7 5   ♡ K   ◇ 10 9 5   ♣ 7 6 5 3

Bid 3◇, which should be thought of as a waiting bid, rather than "Fourth Suit Forcing," because you're already in a game-forcing auction. Your four small clubs are not adequate support to raise opener's *minor.* **If opener has three spades, you want to make it easy for him to support your major.** If instead, opener bids 3♡ to show 6-7 hearts, you should raise to 4♡. If he bids 3NT, you will pass. You plan to support clubs *only* if partner rebids them.

2.   ♠ Q 10 8 7   ♡ 7   ◇ K J 9 8 6 3   ♣ J 4

Bid 3NT. You are not interested in hearing anything more about partner's hand. If opener has three diamonds, is it possible that you belong in diamonds? Certainly, but there's no point in bidding 3◇ – the bid does not promise a long, strong suit. Therefore, simply bid the cheapest game. Who knows, maybe you'll get lucky and West will lead the unbid suit.

3.   ♠ 9 8 6 4 ♡ Q 7 ◊ A 6 5 2 ♣ Q 6 5

Bid 3♡. **With many hands that contain a decent doubleton in opener's first-bid suit, responder should take a preference to that suit.** The ball is now back in partner's court.

4.   ♠ K J 9 5 4 ♡ Q 10 ◊ 7 ♣ 9 8 7 4 3

Bid 3♡, not 4♣. You are not ready to give up on either major suit. If opener has a good heart suit and bids 4♡, you should pass without any regrets. If opener bids 3♠, you'll bid 4♠. Finally, if opener bids 3NT, *then and only then* will you show your support by bidding 4♣.

5.   ♠ K Q 9 7 5 ♡ A J 6 ◊ 8 6 ♣ 9 7 4

Bid 4♡. Because a 3♡ preference promises neither support nor a decent hand, you need to jump with hands like this. If all opener needs for slam is 11-ish points and 3-card heart support, he is more than welcome to bid on.

6.   ♠ A 7 5 3 ♡ 7 ◊ 6 5 2 ♣ A J 10 9 7

Bid 4♣. Finally, a hand where you're eager to support clubs. Not only are you confident that you belong in clubs, but slam prospects are bright. If opener cue-bids 4◊ or 4♡, you will cue-bid 4♠ and hope that partner can take control.

West	North	East	South
—	1♡	Pass	1♠
Pass	3♣	Pass	???

7.　　♠ 9 7 6 4　♡ —　◇ 8 5 3 2　♣ K Q J 7 5

Bid 5♣. You usually try to avoid bypassing 4NT. The only justification for this weak "fast arrival" jump to the five level is that you want to show:

- great trump support (5+ cards with strength),
- no interest in either major, and
- a minimum hand with no aces.

Why, specifically, zero aces? If partner is interested in slam, he needs to know the ace situation once you have deprived him of the opportunity to bid Blackwood.

8.　　♠ K Q J 10 9 4　♡ K　◇ 8 6 4 3　♣ 7 4

Bid 4♠ to show a mild slam try with an independent suit. Opener should now be well-placed to evaluate slam chances.

9.　　♠ Q 7 6 4 3 2　♡ A Q　◇ 8 5　♣ A Q 9

Bid 3♡, not 3♠. Unless opener has three spades, you would rather not play in 6♠. **When you're on your way to slam, be wary of weak suits.**

10.　　♠ A Q 7 6 5 3　♡ J　◇ 8 7 5 4　♣ 7 6

Bid 3♠. Were you wondering if I'd ever make this bid?

	North
Contract: 6♡	♠ A Q 10 6 5
Lead: ◇Q	♡ Q J 10
	◇ 4 2
	♣ J 6 4

East (You)
♠ K J 7 4
♡ 6 4 2
◇ A 8 7 6 5
♣ 10

West	*North*	*East*	*South*
—	—	—	1♡
Pass	1♠	Pass	3♣
Pass	4♡	Pass	4NT
Pass	5◇	Pass	6♡
All Pass			

You win the opening lead of the ◇Q with your ace, as South drops the nine.

Question 1: What is your analysis?

Question 2: What would you lead at trick 2?

P.S: Don't be nervous. Only a slam is at stake.

Question 1: What is your analysis?

Answer: If South began with two spades, sooner or later he'll take the spade finesse and go down. Therefore, assume he has only one.

Don't bother dreaming of a club ruff. For his jump to 6♡, declarer must have the ♣A along with the ♡AK.

If declarer wants to ruff a diamond in dummy, you can't stop him. What *can* you stop him from doing? **If he needs to set up dummy's fifth spade by using dummy's three trump entries, you can prevent *that*!**

Question 2: What would you lead at trick 2?

Answer: The correct lead is a trump, which removes one of dummy's entries. At this point, South can't set up dummy's fifth spade and can no longer make 6♡.

If you lead a minor suit at trick 2, declarer will win the trick and continue as follows:

Trick 3: Lead the ♠8 to dummy's ace.
Trick 4: Ruff a spade with the ♡8.
Trick 5: Lead the ♡3 to dummy's ♡10.
Trick 6: Ruff another spade with the ♡9.
Trick 7: Lead the ♡5 to dummy's ♡J.
Trick 8: Ruff a spade, which removes East's ♠K.
Trick 9: Lead ♡7 to ♡Q, which also draws trumps.
Trick 10: Cash dummy's last spade and discard the ♣9.

Here is the entire deal:

North

Contract: 6♡
Lead: ◇Q

♠ A Q 10 6 5
♡ Q J 10
◇ 4 2
♣ J 6 4

West
♠ 9 3 2
♡ —
◇ Q J 10 3
♣ Q 8 7 5 3 2

East (You)
♠ K J 7 4
♡ 6 4 2
◇ A 8 7 6 5
♣ 10

South
♠ 8
♡ A K 9 8 7 5 3
◇ K 9
♣ A K 9

West	North	East	South
—	—	—	1♡
Pass	1♠	Pass	3♣
Pass	4♡	Pass	4NT
Pass	5◇	Pass	6♡
All Pass			

Partner Doubles and RHO Raises

For each of the hands below, the auction has begun:

West	North	East	South
1◇	Dbl	2◇	???

East's raise to 2◇ relieves you of the obligation to respond to partner's takeout double. Even so, you don't need a lot to make a "free bid" – just something worth talking about.

If South wants to compete, but is not sure what to bid, he can make a Responsive Double. This very flexible call forces the doubler to bid. As a valuable weapon, it should be in *every* partnership's arsenal.

As South, evaluate each hand and decide what to do. Only your side is vulnerable.

1. ♠ 10 7 6 4 ♡ 10 7 6 4 ◇ A 8 ♣ K 7 5
2. ♠ 7 4 ♡ K Q 10 6 ◇ 6 3 ♣ 7 6 4 3 2
3. ♠ K Q 8 ♡ 7 5 4 3 ◇ A 8 ♣ 9 7 5 2
4. ♠ 7 4 ♡ 6 3 ◇ 8 6 5 3 ♣ A Q J 10 8
5. ♠ 5 4 ♡ 8 7 4 ◇ K Q 10 ♣ A J 8 7 6
6. ♠ K 2 ♡ 8 6 5 3 ◇ K Q J 9 8 ♣ 5 4
7. ♠ A Q 9 7 5 ♡ 7 ◇ 8 4 3 ♣ Q 10 7 6
8. ♠ A 7 ♡ K 9 5 2 ◇ 6 ♣ A 10 9 7 5 3
9. ♠ A 10 7 6 3 ♡ A 9 8 4 2 ◇ 8 ♣ 7 5
10. ♠ 8 6 ♡ 7 4 ◇ K 2 ♣ A K 10 7 6 4 3

West	North	East	South
1♢	Dbl	2♢	???

1.   ♠ 10 7 6 4   ♡ 10 7 6 4   ♢ A 8   ♣ K 7 5

Double. A perfect Responsive Double. You are happy to play in the major of partner's choice.

2.   ♠ 7 4   ♡ K Q 10 6   ♢ 6 3   ♣ 7 6 4 3 2

Bid 2♡. You have enough to throw your two cents in, and if the opponents buy the contract, you've made it easy for your partner to lead a heart. **After partner makes a takeout double, you don't need a 5-card suit to make a free bid.**

3.   ♠ K Q 8   ♡ 7 5 4 3   ♢ A 8   ♣ 9 7 5 2

Double, which is a lot more flexible than bidding 2♡, and you certainly don't want to tell partner to lead hearts. If partner bids 2♠, you won't be embarrassed to table your ♠K Q 8.

4.   ♠ 7 4   ♡ 6 3   ♢ 8 6 5 3   ♣ A Q J 10 8

Bid 3♣. I'm not thrilled to be at the three level, vulnerable, but I am always impressed by a strong suit. I don't want to defend 2♢; and once again, I'm eager to ensure the best lead if West becomes declarer.

5.   ♠ 5 4   ♡ 8 7 4   ◇ K Q 10   ♣ A J 8 7 6

Bid 2NT to invite game. This bid is more constructive than 3♣. You want partner to raise with about 14 HCP. If he passes 2NT, you expect eight tricks in notrump to be no more difficult than nine in clubs.

6.   ♠ K 2   ♡ 8 6 5 3   ◇ K Q J 9 8   ♣ 5 4

Pass. Don't bid 2♡ or 2NT and let the opposition off the hook. Your opponents are about to play a diamond contract, which is just fine with you. You can't make a penalty double – but a little patience is likely to go a long way. Partner is probably void in diamonds, and will have no interest in selling out when 2◇ is passed around to him. With his 3-suited hand, he is almost certain to reopen by making a second takeout double. He may be surprised when you pass, but with your 24-carat diamonds, defending 2◇ doubled is as good as it gets.

7.   ♠ A Q 9 7 5   ♡ 7   ◇ 8 4 3   ♣ Q 10 7 6

Bid 3♠. With your promising 5-4-3-1 distribution, and no wasted values in the enemy suit, a nonjump bid of 2♠ does not do justice to this hand. If partner has extra values, he'll have no problem raising to game. You hope that he'll also accept your invitation with any hand that includes four spades and a singleton diamond.

West	North	East	South
1◇	Dbl	2◇	???

8.   ♠ A 7   ♡ K 9 5 2   ◇ 6   ♣ A 10 9 7 5 3
Cue-bid 3◇. After partner's takeout double, a cue-bid
shows unexpected strength. Once East raises, you
could make a Responsive Double with a good balanced
hand, so *this* cue-bid suggests diamond shortness.
It also suggests a long club suit; if you had a strong
hand with a long major, you would jump to game.

If partner bids 3♡, you'll settle for 4♡. Slam might
be laydown, but only wide-eyed optimists base their
bidding on the hope that partner has the perfect hand.
If partner responds 3♠, you will jump to 5♣.

9.   ♠ A 10 7 6 3   ♡ A 9 8 4 2   ◇ 8   ♣ 7 5
Bid 4◇! "Normal" cue-bids are nonjumps and show
general strength. But *this* unusual (yet logical) jump
cue-bid is *very* specific. It tells partner to bid game in
his longer/stronger major. After his vulnerable takeout
double, it's hard to imagine any hand for partner that
doesn't offer a good play for game.

10.   ♠ 8 6   ♡ 7 4   ◇ K 2   ♣ A K 10 7 6 4 3
Bid 3NT. On a diamond lead, you expect to take eight
tricks in your own hand. Partner's double must include
strength in hearts and spades – where else could it be?

Contract: 4♠
Lead: ◇K

North
♠ A K Q 3
♡ Q 5 3
◇ 7 4
♣ A J 9 6

South
♠ J 10 9 6 5 2
♡ J 8 7 6
◇ A 5
♣ 5

West	North	East	South
1◇	Dbl	2◇	3♠
Pass	4♠	All Pass	

Your jump to 3♠ showed excellent appreciation of your 6-4 distribution opposite partner's takeout double.

Question 1: How many tricks might you lose?

Question 2: Which suit are you afraid to lead?

Question 3: What is your plan?

Question 4: After winning the ◇K lead with your ◇A, what would you lead at trick 2?

Question 1: How many tricks might you lose?

Answer: One diamond and three heart tricks. The missing ♡10 is a major problem.

Question 2: Which suit are you afraid to lead?

Answer: Hearts. If you lead hearts, you will probably lose *three* heart tricks. With correct defense, this is true regardless of whether North or South breaks the suit, or if you lead a low card or an honor. However, if you can force E-W to lead hearts (after trumps are drawn), and play second-hand low, you'll lose only *two* heart tricks.

Question 3: What is your plan?

Answer: Use dummy's trumps to eliminate North's clubs as well as draw trumps. Once you finish the clubs, throw E-W in with your inevitable diamond loser. The opponent who wins must lead hearts or give a ruff-sluff. A nice strip and endplay.

Question 4: After winning the ◇K lead with your ◇A, what would you lead at trick 2?

Answer: Lead a club to the ace. Then,
Trick 3:   Ruff a club with the ♠J.
Trick 4:   Lead a trump to dummy's ace.
Trick 5:   Ruff a club with the ♠10.
Trick 6:   Lead a trump to dummy's king.
Trick 7:   Ruff dummy's last club in your hand.
Trick 8:   Exit with your ◇5. Well done!

Here is the entire deal:

North

Contract: 4♠   ♠ A K Q 3
Lead: ◇K   ♡ Q 5 3
                  ◇ 7 4
                  ♣ A J 9 6

West		*East*
♠ 7		♠ 8 4
♡ A 10 4		♡ K 9 2
◇ K Q 8 6 2		◇ J 10 9 3
♣ K 8 3 2		♣ Q 10 7 4

South
♠ J 10 9 6 5 2
♡ J 8 7 6
◇ A 5
♣ 5

West	*North*	*East*	*South*
1◇	Dbl	2◇	3♠
Pass	4♠	All Pass	

For each of the hands below, the auction has begun:

West	North	East	South
—	—	Pass	1♦
1♡	Dbl	Pass	???

North's Negative Double promises 6+ HCP and exactly 4 spades. It says nothing about clubs.

As South, evaluate each hand and decide what to do. Neither side is vulnerable.

1. ♠ A K   ♡ 8 7 5 4   ♦ 9 7 5 4 2   ♣ A Q

2. ♠ A Q 10   ♡ 8 7 5 4   ♦ A Q 5 3   ♣ 7 6

3. ♠ A Q 5 3   ♡ 8 5   ♦ A K 7 5 4   ♣ 6 3

4. ♠ K 10 8 2   ♡ 9   ♦ A K Q 7 6   ♣ Q J 4

5. ♠ 8 6 5   ♡ 6 4   ♦ K 6 5 4 2   ♣ A K Q

6. ♠ A 4   ♡ A 5   ♦ K Q 10 7 5   ♣ A Q 9 6

7. ♠ 5 2   ♡ 4   ♦ A K 9 5 4   ♣ A K J 7 4

8. ♠ A Q   ♡ Q J 6   ♦ K J 7 6   ♣ A Q 4 3

9. ♠ K   ♡ A 8   ♦ A K Q 9 8 6 5   ♣ 10 7 6

10. ♠ J 4   ♡ Q   ♦ K J 10 9 5 4   ♣ A K 7 6

After Partner's Negative Double

West	North	East	South
—	—	Pass	1♦
1♡	Dbl	Pass	???

1. ♠ A K ♡ 8 7 5 4 ◇ 9 7 5 4 2 ♣ A Q

Bid 1NT. You're not supposed to bid notrump without a stopper in the enemy suit; but on this hand, you don't have any plausible alternative. **In reality, on some competitive auctions, you might have to bid 1NT or even 2NT with no stopper in the opponent's suit!** If responder has a strong hand and wants to raise your 1NT bid to 3NT but lacks a stopper, he can cue-bid 2♡ to ask "how are your hearts?" If he passes 1NT and has no stopper, you're only in one, so no big deal.

2. ♠ A Q 10 ♡ 8 7 5 4 ◇ A Q 5 3 ♣ 7 6

Bid 1♠. With these cards, bidding your chunky 3-card spade suit feels like a smaller fib than 1NT. Although Negative Doubles is an excellent and essential convention, you must accept that a double can sometimes create terrible rebid problems for the opener. When that happens, you'll just have to improvise as best you can.

3. ♠ A Q 5 3 ♡ 8 5 ◇ A K 7 5 4 ♣ 6 3

Bid 2♠. Finally, a hand where you don't have to lie. After partner makes a negative double, this bid is *not* a game-forcing jump-shift. It's just a "sign of life," showing 4 spades and a better hand than if you bid 1♠.

4. ♠ K 10 8 2 ♡ 9 ◇ A K Q 7 6 ♣ Q J 4

Bid 3♠, the same invitational bid you would make if
partner responded 1♠. **A singleton in the opponent's
suit is always wonderful.**

5. ♠ 8 6 5 ♡ 6 4 ◇ K 6 5 4 2 ♣ A K Q

Bid 2♣. Uh oh, here we go again with the fibs.
I do understand that you're not happy introducing a
3-card suit that partner never promised. Neither am I.
Here are the alternatives. Can you find a better one?

• 1♠ with ♠8 6 5. Yuck! How would you feel
  if partner has a good hand and raises?

• 1NT with ♡6 4. Hmmm.

• 2◇ on ◇K 6 5 4 2. No thanks. If responder
  passes and tables a singleton diamond, you'll
  soon be cured of rebidding suits like this one.
  Now you know why I bid 2♣.

6. ♠ A 4 ♡ A 5 ◇ K Q 10 7 5 ♣ A Q 9 6

Cue-bid 2♡. **When responder makes a Negative
Double, opener's cue-bid is game-forcing.** The bid
shows a hand strong enough to force to game opposite
a 6-count and says nothing about hearts (or spades).
Any distribution is possible.

West	*North*	*East*	*South*
—	—	Pass	1♢
1♡	Dbl	Pass	???

7.   ♠ 5 2   ♡ 4   ♢ A K 9 5 4   ♣ A K J 7 4

Bid 3♣. Another "sign of life" jump in an unbid suit that is invitational rather than forcing. You are not strong enough to make a game-forcing cue-bid. **Any time partner makes an "I want you to bid" double, such as takeout or negative, only a cue-bid is forcing and all jumps are invitational.**

8.   ♠ A Q   ♡ Q J 6   ♢ K J 7 6   ♣ A Q 4 3

Bid 2NT, just as you planned to bid if partner responded 1♡ or 1♠. Because this jump promises a balanced hand with 18-19 HCP, there's no need to jump to 3NT.

9.   ♠ K   ♡ A 8   ♢ A K Q 9 8 6 5   ♣ 10 7 6

Bid 3NT. The only type of hand that should make the double jump to 3NT is a strong hand with a long suit and a stopper in the overcaller's suit. If you're nervous about a sneak attack in clubs – don't worry, be happy.

10.   ♠ J 4   ♡ Q   ♢ K J 10 9 5 4   ♣ A K 7 6

Bid 2♢, planning to compete with 3♣ if an opponent bids 2♡. There is no absolute rule as to how to rebid with 6-4 hands, but your diamond intermediates suggest emphasizing that suit.

Contract: 3NT
Lead: ♡K

North
♠ 10 9 4 3
♡ 8 6 4
◇ J
♣ A K J 8 7

South
♠ A Q
♡ A 7 5 2
◇ A Q 9 8
♣ Q 10 5

West	North	East	South
—	—	Pass	1◇
1♡	Dbl	Pass	2NT
Pass	3NT	All Pass	

Here are the first four tricks:

Trick 1: West wins the ♡K and East follows.

Trick 2: West continues with the ♡Q.
East discards the ♣2, and you win the ♡A.

Trick 3: You cash the ♣Q.

Trick 4: You cash the ♣10, and West discards the ◇5.

Question 1: How many winners do you have?

Question 2: Can you be sure of a ninth trick?

Question 3: What do you lead at trick 5?

Question 1: How many winners do you have?

Answer: Eight tricks – five clubs and three aces.

Question 2: Can you be sure of a ninth trick?

Answer: At trick 1, you couldn't be sure. However, when West showed out of clubs at the fourth trick, your contract is assured.

Question 3: What do you lead at trick 5?

Answer: A heart. Instead of taking a finesse, endplay West. Once he finishes running his hearts, he'll be forced to lead a spade or diamond into your pair of AQ's. Now that you know West is out of clubs, the stage is set.

What trap must you avoid?
It would be soooooooo easy to make the mistake of running clubs. Unfortunately, if you then throw West in, *you* will be squeezed when he cashes his last heart at trick 10. You will be sitting with ♠AQ and ◇AQ, and will be forced to discard one of your queens, which will spoil everything.

Although everyone loves a good squeeze,
Marty Sez: Squeezing someone else is fun; squeezing yourself is not.

Here is the entire deal:

North

Contract: 3NT ♠ 10 9 4 3

Lead: ♡K ♡ 8 6 4

♢ J

♣ A K J 8 7

West	*East*
♠ J 6 5	♠ K 8 7 2
♡ K Q J 10 3	♡ 9
♢ K 7 6 5	♢ 10 4 3 2
♣ 9	♣ 6 4 3 2

South

♠ A Q

♡ A 7 5 2

♢ A Q 9 8

♣ Q 10 5

West	*North*	*East*	*South*
—	—	Pass	1♢
1♡	Dbl	Pass	2NT
Pass	3NT	All Pass	

OBAR-BIDS

West	You	East	Partner
1♡	Pass	2♡	Pass
Pass	???		

Everyone knows how critical it is to "push 'em up" when the opponents are about to play at the two level with a fit. In the *pass-out* seat, it is quite safe for you to balance. E-W have a fit, so your side almost certainly does also. They have limited strength, so your side has roughly half the deck. Whatever strength you don't have *must* be in partner's hand.

However, "because they have a fit, we have a fit." I've always believed that the player in the *direct seat* should also be eager and free to compete with less than traditional values if he has something worth saying. In the auction above, your partner is said to be in the direct seat because his RHO bid.

Another reason for partner to strive to bid in the direct seat is to help *you* on opening lead. West is likely to become declarer; so if partner has a strong suit, you'd *love* to hear about it.

Many years ago, I invented an acronym to describe this philosophy of "pre-balancing." I call the technique "OBAR-BIDS." It stands for: **O**pponents **B**id **A**nd **R**aise, **B**alance **I**n **D**irect **S**eat.

Question 1: In addition to 1♡ – Pass – 2♡, on what other auctions do OBAR-BIDS apply?

Answer: Any auction when an opponent opens 1 of a suit and his partner raises to 2.

Question 2: Does it matter if the opponents are playing Inverted Minors, which means that responder's raise is strong and forcing?

Answer: Yes and no. Because you don't need to be concerned about the opponents *stealing* the contract at the two level, you are less likely to double "light." However, if you have a long strong suit, you should be even more eager to make a lead-directing overcall to help partner find the best lead.

Question 3: Does anything change if your side is vulnerable?

Answer: No. The philosophy of OBAR-BIDS is unchanged, although you should be careful.

Question 4: When partner OBAR-BIDS, what must I keep in mind?

Answer: Don't *bury* him. Remember that partner did not promise a strong hand. If the opposition bids on, go quietly unless you have exceptional distribution – and be grateful that partner balanced.

On each of the hands below, the auction has begun:

West	North	East	South
1♡	Pass	2♡	???

Assume that you've agreed, at least for the time being, to play OBAR-BIDS. As South, in the direct seat, evaluate each hand and decide what to do.
The opponents are vulnerable, your side is not.

1. ♠ K 9 8 5   ♡ 6   ◇ A 10 6 4   ♣ Q 10 8 6

2. ♠ K J 5   ♡ Q 7 6   ◇ K J 6 3   ♣ K Q 6

3. ♠ K Q J 9 6   ♡ 3   ◇ Q 9 8 5   ♣ 7 4 2

4. ♠ 8 6 4   ♡ 9 5   ◇ A Q J 10 7 6   ♣ 6 3

5. ♠ 10 7 6 4 3   ♡ K J 2   ◇ A 2   ♣ K Q 4

6. ♠ 7 4   ♡ 2   ◇ K J 6 5 3   ♣ A 10 9 5 2

7. ♠ Q J 7 6 5   ♡ 4 2   ◇ A   ♣ K 9 5 3 2

8. ♠ K Q J 9 6 4 2   ♡ 9 4   ◇ 7   ♣ 8 4 2

9. ♠ A K Q 9   ♡ 8 6 5 2   ◇ 5   ♣ A 10 9 2

10. ♠ A 7 3 2   ♡ A 5   ◇ J 9 8 7 5   ♣ A 3

West	North	East	South
1♡	Pass	2♡	???

1. ♠ K 9 8 5 ♡ 6 ◊ A 10 6 4 ♣ Q 10 8 6

Double. With your singleton, this hand is ideal for a light OBAR-BIDS takeout double despite having only 9 HCP. If you pass, you run the risk that 2♡ will be passed out when partner has too many hearts to balance. **When short in the opponent's suit, be very aggressive.**

2. ♠ K J 5 ♡ Q 7 6 ◊ K J 6 3 ♣ K Q 6

Pass. Points, Schmoints! You may be impressed with these 15 HCP, but I am not. Why do I hate this hand?

- 4-3-3-3 is the worst possible distribution.
- Too many jacks, and no aces or intermediates.
- Your queen in their suit is probably useless.

If West bids, you'll be happy that you didn't broadcast your HCP. If West passes and partner balances, that's okay. If 2♡ is passed out – no regrets. **Be cautious with balanced hands in competitive auctions.**

3. ♠ K Q J 9 6 ♡ 3 ◊ Q 9 8 5 ♣ 7 4 2

Bid 2♠. A minimum but ideal hand for OBAR-BIDS. You'd love to get a spade lead, and don't want to risk defending 2♡. You have more offense than defense, so if partner wants to raise spades, that's okay.

4.   ♠ 8 6 4   ♡ 9 5   ◇ A Q J 10 7 6   ♣ 6 3
Bid 3◇. You prefer having a 6-card suit for a light
overcall, especially at the three level with no short suit.
If you would pass because you had *only* 7 HCP,
Marty Sez: Any player unwilling to bid 3◇ and help
partner on opening lead should be condemned to a
lifetime of opening leads without any sequences!

5.   ♠ 10 7 6 4 3   ♡ K J 2   ◇ A 2   ♣ K Q 4
Pass. Although I love to make OBAR-BIDS, I'm not
even tempted here. Why? I have a flat hand with
terrible spades and questionable heart honors. The fact
that I would have opened the bidding is *not* relevant.

6.   ♠ 7 4   ♡ 2   ◇ K J 6 5 3   ♣ A 10 9 5 2
Bid 2NT (Unusual NT) to show the minors. It is silly
to treat 2NT as a natural notrump bid *here*. Even if you
have enough points to bid 2NT (natural), partner must
be broke, and down you'll go. Your 5-5 shape justifies
competing to the three level in partner's longer minor.
Also, if opener jumps to 4♡, your bid may enable
partner to sacrifice based on the favorable vulnerability.

7.   ♠ Q J 7 6 5   ♡ 4 2   ◇ A   ♣ K 9 5 3 2
Bid 2♠. A 3♡ Michaels Cue-Bid is out of the question
with this modest hand. If partner hates spades, you'd
be at the four level! On an auction like this, you would
need a terrific hand to cue-bid. Content yourself by
bidding your major suit.

West	North	East	South
1♡	Pass	2♡	???

8. ♠ K Q J 9 6 4 2 ♡ 9 4 ◇ 7 ♣ 8 4 2

Bid 3♠ with this textbook preempt. If West bids 4♡, your descriptive bid should make it easy for partner to decide whether or not to sacrifice.

9. ♠ A K Q 9 ♡ 8 6 5 2 ◇ 5 ♣ A 10 9 2

Bid 2♠, your 4-card suit notwithstanding. E-W must have 8-9 hearts, and with your four cards, partner can't have more than one. If he happens to have *good* support, you could even have a game.

10. ♠ A 7 3 2 ♡ A 5 ◇ J 9 8 7 5 ♣ A 3

Here are your choices, each of which is greatly flawed:

- Pass: not very ambitious with a promising hand.

- Double: you have only two clubs.

- 2♠: Overcalling this suit is going too far.

- 3◇: The suit is weak, and you could miss a spade fit.

What's the answer? I would double, based on agreeing to play Equal Level Conversion Doubles (ELCD). When playing ELCD, if you double 2♡ and partner bids 3♣, you can bid 3◇ without showing extra values! Of course, on a good day, partner will bid spades or diamonds.

OBAR-BIDS

		North	
Contract: 4♠		♠ 10 6 5	
Lead: ◇9		♡ 10 3	
		◇ 7 4 2	
		♣ A Q J 5 3	

East (You)
♠ 8
♡ 9 8 6 5
◇ A K Q 8 6
♣ 7 4 2

West	*North*	*East* (You)	*South*
—	—	—	1♠
Pass	2♠	3◇	4♠
All Pass			

After your helpful lead-directing 3◇ overcall, partner obediently leads the ◇9. You win the first three tricks with high diamonds. On the third round, partner discards the discouraging ♡2.

Question 1: What suit might provide the setting trick?

Question 2: What would you lead at trick 4?

By the way: What holding in West's hand will ensure defeating the contract?

Question 1: What suit might provide the setting trick?

Answer: Spades. Very often, the way to solve bridge problems is the process of elimination. Regardless of who has the ♣K, that suit offers no hope. Partner's ♡2 said that he didn't like hearts. Therefore, your only hope is to try to promote a trump trick for your partner.

Question 2: What would you lead at trick 4?

Answer: You should lead a diamond. Once you do, whether South ruffs high or low, he can't shut out partner's ♠J 7 2. If you were reluctant to lead a fourth diamond because you'd be giving a ruff-sluff, Marty Sez: **When declarer's side has no losers in any side suit, be eager to give a ruff-sluff.**

By the way: What holding in West's hand will ensure defeating the contract?

Answer: In addition to the actual ♠Jxx, your defense would have been equally successful if West had the ♠Qx or ♠K. Whether or not you knew this answer, if you led a diamond, well done!

Also worth noting: If you had held West's cards, would you have made the well-thought-out discard of the ♡2? As long as East could be persuaded that hearts were hopeless, he should lead a diamond, and the ♠J was as good as gold.

Here is the entire deal:

Contract: 4♠
Lead: ◇9

North
♠ 10 6 5
♡ 10 3
◇ 7 4 2
♣ A Q J 5 3

West
♠ J 7 2
♡ K Q 7 4 2
◇ 9 3
♣ 10 8 6

East (You)
♠ 8
♡ 9 8 6 5
◇ A K Q 8 6
♣ 7 4 2

South
♠ A K Q 9 4 3
♡ A J
◇ J 10 5
♣ K 9

West	*North*	*East* (You)	*South*
			1♠
Pass	2♠	3◇	4♠
All Pass			

LAST BUT NOT LEAST

The first three of these segments include
page numbers for easy reference.

Bergenisms:
Tips You Can Take to the Bank

A summary of useful tips from the seven chapters.
While the chapters deal with specific auctions, these
"words to the wise" have been modified to apply in a
variety of situations.

Glossary Plus

A description of the conventions used in this book,
along with definitions of terms.

Calling All Cue-Bids

A complete listing of all five types of cue-bids that
appear in BBBQ1, with descriptions of each.

To Alert or Not to Alert

Based on ACBL guidelines as of September 2003, this
page states which bids are alertable and which are not.

Highly Recommended

Everything you need to improve your game, from books
to interactive CDs.

Chapter 1 - Rebidding After a Transfer

Chapter 2 - We Bid Three Suits

Chapter 3 - After Opener Raises Your Major

Page #

25 Opener might raise responder's major
with 3-card support. On some hands,
he should be delighted to raise with three;
on others, he will raise because there are
no alternatives.

26 When opener raises your major, jumping
to game with only a 4-card suit is rarely
correct.

26 After opener raises your major,
responder's bid of a new suit is forcing
for one round, and preserves all options.

27 Even a weak 6-card suit looks a whole lot
better once partner supports that suit.
And if you have a 4-card suit on the side,
don't forget "6-4, bid more."

27 Honors in the trump suit are more
valuable than honors in the side suits.

Chapter 4 - Opener has Jump-Shifted

Page #

33 Opener's jump-shift may include as many as 6-7 cards in his first suit, and as few as 3 cards in his second suit.

34 After opener's jump-shift, responder's bid of the fourth suit is an artificial, waiting bid.

34 When responder has a 5-card major, the best way to find out if opener has 3-card support is to make an economical, flexible bid.

35 With many hands that contain a decent doubleton in opener's first-bid suit, responder should take a preference to that suit.

35 When opener jump-shifts into a minor suit, responder should be reluctant to raise that suit.

36 If slam is possible, avoid jumping to the five level (because you are bypassing 4NT).

36 If you're on your way to slam, avoid bidding weak suits.

Page #

41 You don't need a lot to make a "free bid;" just something worth talking about.

41 If the opponents bid and raised a suit and partner has bid or doubled, sometimes you would like to compete but are not sure what to bid. The solution is to make a Responsive Double. This very flexible call is the equivalent of a takeout double, and should be a valuable weapon in every partnership's arsenal.

42 After partner makes a takeout double, you don't need a 5-card suit to make a free bid.

43 Don't disturb the opponents when they are about to play in your best suit.

44 After partner's takeout double, a cue-bid shows unexpected strength.

44 Only wide-eyed optimists base their bidding on the hope that partner has the perfect hand.

44 When partner makes a takeout double, he usually has stoppers in the unbid suits.

50 Don't bid notrump without a stopper in the enemy suit. However, on some competitive auctions, you might *have* to bid 1NT or even 2NT with no stopper in the opponent's suit!

50 Negative Doubles are essential, but responder's double may create terrible rebid problems for opener.

50 After partner makes a negative double, a jump in a new suit is *not* a game-forcing jump-shift. It's just a "sign of life."

51 A singleton in the opponent's suit is always wonderful.

51 When responder makes a Negative Double, opener's cue-bid is game-forcing.

52 If partner makes an "I want you to bid" double, such as takeout or negative, jumps are invitational and a cue-bid is forcing.

52 Opener's double jump to 3NT shows a long minor suit and a strong, unbalanced hand.

52 There is no absolute rule as to how to rebid with 6-4 hands, so it makes sense to be influenced by your intermediate cards.

Page #

57 It is critical to not sell out cheaply when the opponents are about to play at the two level with a fit.

57 "When they have a fit, we have a fit." The player in the direct seat can compete with less than traditional values if he has something worth saying.

57 An excellent reason to strive to bid in the direct seat is to help partner with his opening lead.

60 When you're short in the opponent's suit, be very aggressive.

60 Be cautious with balanced hands in competitive auctions.

61 The fact that you would have opened is not relevant when deciding whether to take action after an opponent opens.

61 After your opponents bid and raise hearts:

- an overcall of 2NT shows the minors, as opposed to a hand that wants to play in 2NT.
- You would need a terrific hand to make a Michaels Cue-Bid of 3♡.

GLOSSARY PLUS

Balancing Seat (Pass-out Seat) – page 57
If your pass would end the auction, try to *reopen* rather
than allow the enemy to play in a low-level contract.

Direct Seat – pages 57, 59
Because your RHO took action, partner will still get a
chance to bid even if you pass.

Equal Level Conversion Doubles (ELCD) – page 62
If you double a major suit, then bid diamonds after a club
response, you are *not* showing extra values (by agreement).

5NT, Pick-a-Slam – page 12
A jump to 5NT which asks partner to choose between
a small slam in a suit contract or one in notrump.

Fourth Suit Artificial (and Forcing) – pages 19, 20
After the partnership has bid three suits, responder's bid
of the fourth suit is forcing and says nothing about that suit.

Free Bid – pages 41-42
A bid made after both partner and RHO took action.

Independent Suit – pages 20, 36
A suit that is so long and strong, it doesn't need support.

Inverted Minors – page 58
A convention where responder's raise to 2 is strong
(usually 10+ HCP) and forcing, but a jump to 3 is weak.

Negative Doubles – pages 48-55
Responder's double of a 1♡ overcall shows 6+ HCP
and exactly 4 spades.

Jacoby Transfer – pages 9-15
After partner opens 1NT, a 2♢ bid shows 5+ hearts, while 2♡ promises 5+ spades. Opener must bid responder's suit.

OBAR-BIDS – (**Pre-Balancing**) - pages 57-63
A Bergen acronym to describe competing aggressively in the direct seat after your opponents bid and raise a suit. **O**pponents **B**id **A**nd **R**aise, **B**alance **I**n **D**irect **S**eat.

Proven Honors – page 18, 27
Honor cards that are very likely to be useful. Aces are proven, as are honor cards in partner's suit(s).

Quantitative 4NT – page 11
Raising partner's notrump bid to 4NT invites a slam. The bid does *not* ask for aces (or keycards).

Responsive Double – pages 41-42
A takeout double made after the opponents bid and raise a suit, and partner has bid or doubled.

Splinter Bid – pages 11, 28
A jump into a short suit (0-1 card), promising a fit and values for game (or slam). If partner didn't support you, the unusual jump is called a **Self-Splinter** (page 11).

Super-Accept – pages 10, 13
With a 4-card fit and a non-minimum hand, opener jumps after partner's Jacoby Transfer.

Unusual Notrump Overcall – page 61
A method of showing length in the two lower unbid suits after an opponent opens.

Calling All Cue-Bids

Cue-bids #2-5 are made in an opponent's suit, and say nothing about that suit.

1. Slam Try – page 35
A bid in a new suit at the four level after the trump suit has been established, which promises a control in that suit and interest in slam.

2. LHO Opens, Partner Doubles, and RHO Raises Opener's Suit – page 44
A cue-bid in the opponents' suit is game-forcing. The bid usually includes shortness in the opponents' suit, and tends to deny a 5-card major.

3. Partner Doubles 1◇, You Jump to 4◇ – page 44
The 4◇ cue-bid promises at least 5-5 in the majors, with enough offense to justify forcing to game.

4. After Partner Negative Doubles – page 51
Opener's cue-bid promises a very strong hand and is forcing to game. Any distribution is possible, but he usually has an unbalanced hand.

5. Michaels Cue-Bid - page 61
An overcall in the opponent's suit that shows at least five cards in each of two suits. After a 1♡ opening bid, the cue-bid promises spades plus one of the minors.

To Alert or Not to Alert (or Announce)

- This page ONLY addresses bidding in BBBQ-1.
- This is based on ACBL guidelines as of September, 2003. They are all subject to change.
- If not listed, no alert (or announcement) is needed.
- All cue-bids in this book are NOT alertable.
- All bids at the 4+ level in this book are NOT alertable.
- When an alert (or announcement) is needed, it is made by the PARTNER of the player who made the bid.

Equal Level Conversion Doubles (ELCD)   NOT alertable

Fourth-Suit Forcing and Artificial   ALERT

Jacoby Transfer   Announce "Jacoby Transfer"

Negative Doubles   NOT alertable

OBAR-BIDS
(If overcalls and doubles may be *very* light)   ALERT

Opener's double jump to 3NT (long minor)   ALERT

Responder's artificial, waiting bid in the fourth suit

1♡	1♠	
3♣	3♢	ALERT

Responsive Doubles   ALERT

Splinter Bids in this book are DELAYED ALERTS.
If your side declares, declarer or dummy must ALERT *after* the auction is completed but *before* the opening lead.

HIGHLY RECOMMENDED

Softcover Books by Marty Bergen
Buy 1, get 1 (equal or lesser price) for half price

Bergen Best Bridge Quizzes, Vol. 1	$7.95
To Open or Not to Open	$6.95
Better Rebidding with Bergen	$7.95
Understanding 1NT Forcing	$5.95
Hand Evaluation: Points, Schmoints!	$7.95
Introduction to Negative Doubles	$6.95
Negative Doubles	$9.95
Better Bidding With Bergen –	
Volume 1: Uncontested Auctions	$11.95
Volume 2: Competitive Bidding	$11.95

Interactive Software by Mike Lawrence
(first five are now also available for Macintosh)

Counting at Bridge		~~$34.95~~	$30
Private Bridge Lessons, Vol. 1		~~$34.95~~	$30
Private Bridge Lessons, Vol. 2		~~$34.95~~	$30
Defense		~~$34.95~~	$30
Two Over One		~~$34.95~~	$30
Conventions	**Special sale!!**	~~$60.00~~	$35

Interactive CDs by Larry Cohen

Play Bridge with Larry Cohen:

Day 1	~~$29.95~~	$26
Day 2	~~$29.95~~	$26
Day 3	~~$29.95~~	$26

Interactive CDs by Kit Woolsey

Cavendish 2000:

Day 1	~~$29.95~~	$26
Days 2-3	~~$29.95~~	$26

Interactive Software by Fred Gitelman

Bridge Master 2000	~~$59.95~~	$48

• • FREE SHIPPING ON ALL SOFTWARE • •
(in the U.S.)

ORDERING INFORMATION

To place your order, call Marty toll-free at
1-800-386-7432
all major credit cards are welcome

Or send a check or money order (U.S. currency), to:

Marty Bergen
9 River Chase Terrace
Palm Beach Gardens, FL 33418-6817

Please include $3.50 (S&H) for each order.

Postage is FREE (in U.S.) if your order includes a CD.